Cybersecurity Maturity Model Certification (CMMC): Companion CUI Marking Guide

Mark A. Russo, CISSP-ISSAP

Former Chief Information Security Officer, Department of Education

Syber-Risk

DEDICATION

This book is dedicated to my supportive instructors and professors at the National Defense University, Washington, DC, and their daily efforts to train and teach the next generation of cyber-warriors of this great Nation.

This is also dedicated to my family, who have been supportive of my endeavors to plunge into writing as not just a hobby but a calling to make the world a better and more secure place.

Syber-Risk
.com

Cybersecurity Maturity Model Certification (CMMC): Companion CUI Marking Guide

by Mark A. Russo

Printed in the United States of America.

2020:

Revision History for the First Edition

Check Out the
<u>Most-Extensive</u> Cybersecurity Blog Site

This is the primary resource of everything, "Cyber."
"The good, the bad, and the ugly of cybersecurity all in one place."

Join us at https://cybersentinel.tech

This free resource is available to everyone interested in the fate and future of cybersecurity in the 21st Century

Syber-Risk

The Controlled Unclassified Information (CUI) Classification, Marking, and Storage Guide

A Supplement to the DOD's Cybersecurity Maturity Model Certification (CMMC) Framework

CMMC: Companion CUI Marking Guide

Contents

PROPER MARKING OF CUI[1]

Security markings and safeguarding is a significant part of being successful in the application of NIST 800-171. Proper marking is not just for the company or agency, but for those not intended or authorized to view CUI. This chapter delineates how to mark all forms of written and electronic media in order to protect sensitive CUI. While it is unlikely a company or business will create CUI, it will be responsible for the legal protections from either administrative, civil, or criminal implications of failing to care for CUI properly. *Do not be careless.*

The CUI Program standardizes how the Executive branch handles unclassified information[2] that does not meet the criteria required for classification under E.O. 13526, "Classified National Security Information," December 29, 2009, or the Atomic Energy Act but must be protected based on law, regulation, or Government-wide policy. Protections involve the safeguards employed while this information is stored or handled by the Executive branch departments or its subordinate agencies.

Before implementation of the CUI Program, agencies employed *ad hoc*, agency-specific policies, procedures, and markings to safeguard and control this information. This information involved privacy, security, proprietary business interests, and law enforcement information. This was highly inefficient and confusing. Subsequent guidance resulted in inconsistent marking and safeguarding of documents that led to unclear or unnecessarily restrictive dissemination policies. Furthermore, it created obstacles to the *best practice* principle of *Information Sharing,* resulting in part from the 9-11 attack of September 11, 2001[3].

Proper markings alert information holders to the presence of CUI and subsequently when portion markings are required. Markings ensure that CUI is identified, and the exact information is appropriately marked for protection. They

---

[1] This chapter is adapted from the National Archives and Records Administration (NARA) information and artifacts regarding the national CUI program.

[2] While the Legislative and Judicial Branch should defer to the Executive Branch for all matters regarding national security protections and markings, it cannot be guaranteed for vendors working with the other two branches of the US government.

[3] One of the major findings of the 9-11 Commission was that the Central Intelligence Agency (CIA) and the Federal Bureau of Investigation (FBI) each had pieces of critical intelligence that may have prevented the attacks. Congress mandated created information sharing efforts—however, the parochial nature of government has not as of yet solved this problem.

alert CUI holders to any dissemination and safeguarding controls. This chapter provides basic marking guidelines for CUI and is written to provide visibility and requisite security to CUI.

Companies, businesses, organizations, agencies, and most specifically, employees must review their organizations' CUI policy before marking any CUI. The handling of CUI must be per **E.O. 13556, "Controlled Unclassified Information," November 4, 2010**, 32 CFR Part 2002 (this link provides a full version https://www.govinfo.gov/content/pkg/CFR-2017-title32-vol6/pdf/CFR-2017-title32-vol6-part2002.pdf) , supplemental guidance published by the government's overall CUI Executive Agent (EA), the National Archive and Records Administration (NARA), and all applicable EA-approved agency policies. This chapter contains guidance on what each marking is, where and how to apply it, and which items are mandatory or optional based on local agency or organization policy.

CUI Banner Markings (Reference 32 CFR 2002.20(b))

Banner markings are the necessary header (and footer) designations alerting individuals with a need-to-know the required restrictions in place to ensure the protection of the information. Banner makings should be seen by individuals to ensure the maximum protection if the information is set out in the open or inadvertently visible to unauthorized individuals. Those individuals charged with the protection of the CUI are administratively responsible for CUI and protection and are subject to disciplinary actions by the agency or company. The following is a list of basic knowledge required by the agency as well as recipient vendors and contractors of the US Government.

- The initial marking for all CUI is the CUI Banner Marking. This is the central marking that appears at the top (and typically, at the bottom) of each page of any document that contains CUI.

- This marking is MANDATORY for all documents containing CUI. The content of the CUI Banner Marking must be inclusive of all CUI within the document and must be the same on each page.

- The Banner Marking should appear as bold capitalized black text and be centered when feasible. (*There are no designated size or font requirements, but we recommend the same font used for the document, and at least four sizes larger for visual prominence).*

- The CUI Banner Marking may include up to three elements:

    1. The CUI Control Marking (mandatory) may consist of either the word "CONTROLLED" or the acronym "CUI."

    2. CUI Category or Subcategory Markings (mandatory for CUI Specified). These are separated from the CUI Control Marking by a double forward-slash (//) When including multiple categories or subcategories in a Banner Marking, they must be alphabetized and are separated by a single forward-slash (/).

    3. Limited Dissemination (LIMDIS) Control Markings are preceded by a double forward-slash (//) to separate them from the rest of the CUI Banner Marking.

    A sample of the CUI Banner Marking may be found below.

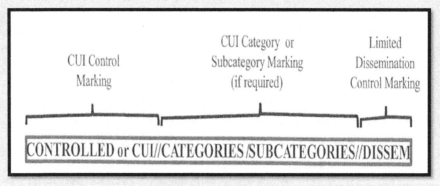

CUI Banner Marking

The above example uses the words "CATEGORIES" and "SUBCATEGORIES" as substitutes for CUI Category or Subcategory Markings and the word "DISSEM" as a substitute for Limited Dissemination Control Marking. Consult the CUI Registry for actual CUI markings.

CUI Banner Control Markings (Reference 32 CFR 2002.20(b)(1))

The CUI Control Marking is mandatory for all CUI and may consist of either the word "CONTROLLED" or the acronym "CUI" (at the designator's discretion). A best practice for CUI Banner Marking includes it being placed at the bottom of the document. Below are two examples showing the options for the CUI Banner Marking.

MANDATORY:
CUI Banner Markings must appear on the top portion of the page.

CONTROLLED

Department of Good Works
Washington, D.C. 20006

August 27, 2016

MEMORANDUM FOR THE DIRECTOR

From: Elliott Alderson, Chief
Robotics Division

Subject: Examples

We support President Walken by ensuring that the Government protects and provides proper access to information to advance the national and public interest.

We lead efforts to standardize and assess the management of classified and controlled unclassified information through oversight, policy development, guidance, education, and reporting.

CONTROLLED

CUI

Department of Good Works
Washington, D.C. 20006

August 27, 2016

MEMORANDUM FOR THE DIRECTOR

From: Tyrell Wellick
Office of the CTO

Subject: Examples

We support President Walken by ensuring that the Government protects and provides proper access to information to advance the national and public interest.

We lead efforts to standardize and assess the management of classified and controlled unclassified information through oversight, policy development, guidance, education, and reporting.

CUI

Optional Best Practice: Also Placed Centered at Bottom

CUI Categories and Subcategories (Reference 32 CFR 2002.12)

The CUI Program is founded on the precondition that only information requiring protection based on law, Federal regulation, or government-wide policy can qualify as CUI. *CUI Categories and Subcategories are necessarily different*. CUI Categories and Subcategories are based on at least one or more laws, regulations, or government-wide policies; these are also referred to as *Authorities*[4] that require a specific type of information to be protected or restricted in its dissemination.

There are two types of CUI Categories and Subcategories: CUI Basic and CUI Specified.

1. ***CUI Basic*** is the standard CUI category. All rules of CUI apply to CUI Basic Categories and Subcategories. This ensures the proper creation and handling of properly marked CUI.

2. ***CUI Specified*** is different since the requirements for how users must treat each type of information vary with each Category or Subcategory. This is because some Authorities have specialized requirements for handling varied types of CUI information.

CUI Specified is NOT a "higher level" of CUI, it is *merely different.* Also, its differences are dictated by law, Federal regulation, or government-wide policy; they cannot be ignored. Furthermore, a document containing multiple CUI Specified Categories and Subcategories must include all of them in the CUI Banner Marking.

There is one additional issue with CUI Specified. Some CUI Categories and Subcategories are only CUI Specified, sometimes based upon the Authorities' local rules or policies. The reason these differences are caused by differing laws or regulations about the same information type; however, only *some* of them may include additional or alternate handling requirements for standard CUI Basic.

Therefore, only CUI created under Authorities would be CUI Specified. Explicitly, if the law, regulation, or Government-wide policy that pertains to an agency are listed in the CUI Registry as a Specified Authority, then you must mark the CUI based on that Authority as CUI Specified and

---

[4] Consider Authorities as local rules or policies that are unique to the particular Federal agency. Typically, the Contract Officer should be able to assist in information briefings with the agency to ensure full compliance by the vendor.

include that marking in the CUI Banner.

The CUI Registry may be found at https://www.archives.gov/cui/registry/category-list

Banner Markings for Category and Subcategory Markings (Reference 32 CFR 2002.20(b)(2))

CUI Category or Subcategory Markings are separated by a double forward-slash (//) from the CUI Control Marking. When including multiple CUI Category or Subcategory Markings in the CUI Banner Marking, they must be separated by a single forward-slash (/). When a document contains CUI Specified, all CUI Specified Category or Subcategory Markings must be included in the CUI Banner Marking.

Additionally, agency heads may approve the use of CUI Basic Category or Subcategory Markings through agency CUI policy. When such agency policy exists, all CUI Basic Category or Subcategory Markings must be included in the CUI Banner Marking.

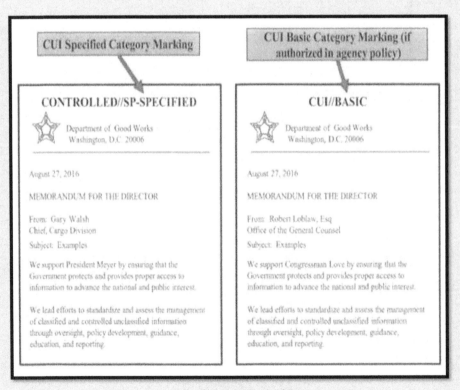

Varied Banner Markings

The above examples use the words "SP-SPECIFIED" and "BASIC" as substitutes for CUI Category and Subcategory Markings. Consult the CUI Registry for actual CUI markings.

Since CUI Specified Categories and Subcategories are different – both from CUI Basic and also from each other – CUI Specified MUST always be included in the CUI Banner. This is done to ensure that every authorized CUI holder and end-user who receives a document containing CUI Specified knows that the document must be treated in a manner that differs from CUI Basic. This is accomplished in two ways:

1. All CUI Specified documents must include the Category or Subcategory marking for all the CUI Specified contained in that document in the CUI Banner Marking. This ensures that initially, a user in receipt of that document is aware of the CUI Banner. This permits the user to be aware of whether they have something other than ordinary CUI Basic. It also allows the user to meet any additional or alternative requirements for the CUI Specified they hold.

2. To ensure that it is evident that a Category or Subcategory is Specified, the marking has "SP-" added to the beginning of the marking after the CUI or Controlled designation.

> **"SP-" added to beginning of Category markings from CUI Registry**

> **MANDATORY:**
> **CUI Specified Markings must appear in CUI Banner**

CONTROLLED/SP-SPECIFIED

★ Department of Good Works
Washington, D.C. 20006

August 27, 2016

MEMORANDUM FOR THE DIRECTOR

From: Elliott Alderson, Chief
Robotics Division

Subject: Examples

We support President Walken by ensuring that the Government protects and provides proper access to information to advance the national and public interest.

We lead efforts to standardize and assess the management of classified and controlled unclassified information through oversight, policy development, guidance, education, and reporting.

CUI/SP-SPECIFIED

★ Department of Good Works
Washington, D.C. 20006

August 27, 2016

MEMORANDUM FOR THE DIRECTOR

From: Tyrell Wellick
Office of the CTO

Subject: Examples

We support President Walken by ensuring that the Government protects and provides proper access to information to advance the national and public interest.

We lead efforts to standardize and assess the management of classified and controlled unclassified information through oversight, policy development, guidance, education, and reporting.

The above examples use the word "SPECIFIED" as a substitute for CUI Category and Subcategory Markings. Consult the CUI Registry for actual CUI markings.

Banner Markings with Multiple of Subcategory Markings (Reference 32 CFR 2002.20)

CUI Specified Markings must precede CUI Basic Markings that were authorized for use by the agency head in the CUI Banner. Consult the agency CUI policy for guidance on the use of CUI Basic Category or Subcategory Markings. Additionally, CUI Category and Subcategory Markings MUST be alphabetized within CUI type (Basic or Specified). Alphabetized Specified CUI categories and subcategories must precede alphabetized Basic CUI categories and subcategories.

Below are examples of CUI Banner Markings used in a document that contains both CUI Specified and CUI Basic.

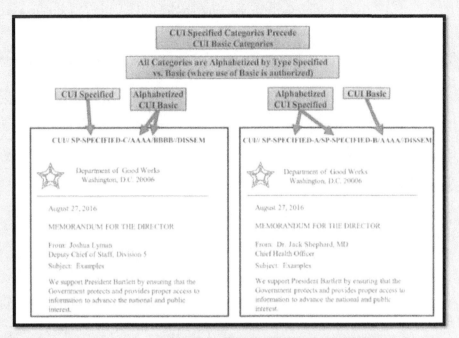

Multiple Category or Subcategory Markings

The above examples use "AAAA" and "BBBB" as substitutes for CUI Basic Category and Subcategory Markings, "SP-SPECIFIED-X" as a substitute for a CUI Specified Category and Subcategory Markings, and "DISSEM" as a substitute for a Limited Dissemination Control Marking. Consult the CUI Registry for actual CUI markings.

Banner Markings (Limited Dissemination Controls)(Reference 32 CFR 2002.20(b)(3)

Only Limited Dissemination (LIMDIS) Control Markings found in the CUI Registry are authorized for use with CUI. Limited Dissemination Control Markings are separated from preceding sections of the CUI Banner Marking by, double forward-slash *(///)*. When a document contains multiple Limited Dissemination Control Markings, those

Limited Dissemination Control Markings MUST be alphabetized and separated from each other with a single forward-slash (/).

Below are examples that show the proper use of Limited Dissemination Control Markings in the CUI Banner Marking in a letter-type document or a slide presentation.

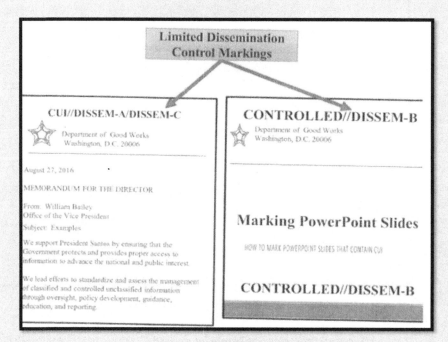

LIMDIS Controls

The above example uses "DISSEM-X" as a substitute for Limited Dissemination Control Markings. Consult the CUI Registry for actual CUI markings.

Designation Indicator (Reference 32 CFR 2002.20(a)(3)(d))

All documents containing CUI must indicate the designator's agency. This may be accomplished with letterhead, a signature block with the agency, or the use of a "Controlled by" line. Every effort should be made to identify a point of contact, branch, or division within an organization responsible for either the creation or protection of the CUI.

Below are examples of Designation Indicators in a slide presentation and a letter-type document.

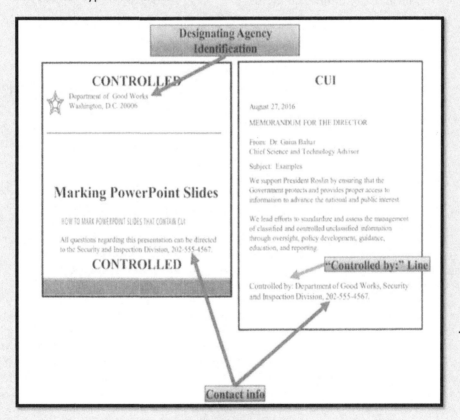

Designation Indicators

Portion Markings (Reference 32 CFR 2002.20(f))

Portion marking of CUI is *optional* in a fully unclassified document but is highly encouraged[5] to facilitate information sharing and proper handling of the information. Agency heads may approve the required use of CUI Portion marking on all CUI generated within their agency. Users should always consult their agency CUI policy when creating CUI documents.

When CUI Portion Marking is used, these rules will be followed. CUI Portion Markings are placed at the beginning of the portion (e.g., beginning of sentence or segment of the CUI), apply it throughout the entire document. CUI Portion Markings are contained within parentheses and may include up to three elements:

1. The CUI Control Marking: This is mandatory when portion marking and must be the acronym "CUI" (the word "Controlled" will not be used in portion marking).

2. CUI Category or Subcategory Markings: These can be found in the CUI Registry.

   a. When used, CUI Category or Subcategory Markings are separated from the CUI Control Marking by a double forward-slash (//).

   b. When including multiple categories or subcategories in a portion, CUI Category or Subcategory Markings are separated from each other by a single forward-slash (/).

3. Limited Dissemination Control Markings: These can be found in the CUI Registry and are separated from preceding CUI markings by a double forward-slash (//). When including multiple Limited Dissemination Control Markings, they must be alphabetized and separated from each other by a single forward-slash (/).

4. When CUI Portion Markings are used, and a portion does not contain CUI, a "U" is placed in parentheses to indicate that the portion contains Uncontrolled Unclassified Information.

---

[5] The author strongly supports the use of portion markings. They further help when providing reports and responding to requests for information from the public; this provides clear boundaries for information release in accordance with the law.

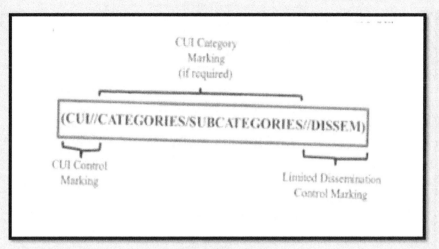

Portion Marking Standards

The above example uses the words "CATEGORIES" and "SUBCATEGORIES" as substitutes for CUI Category or Subcategory Markings and the word "DISSEM" as a substitute for a Limited Dissemination Control Marking. Consult the CUI Registry for actual CUI markings.

The presence of at least one item categorized as CUI in a document requires CUI marking of the entire document. CUI Portion Markings can be of significant assistance in determining if a document contains CUI and, therefore, must be marked appropriately. Additionally, when portion markings are used, and any portion does not contain CUI, a "(U)" is placed in front of that portion to indicate that it contains Uncontrolled or non-CUI -Unclassified[6] Information.

---

[6] Uncontrolled appears to be an ambiguous stamen from NARA; it is best considered as UNCLASSIFIED information that can be freely shared with the general public.

CUI Portion Markings

CONTROLLED

Department of Good Works
Washington, D.C. 20006

August 27, 2016

MEMORANDUM FOR THE DIRECTOR

From: Sydney Wade
Chief, Environmental Protection Division

Subject: (CUI) Traffic Patterns of Dupont Circle

(U) We support President Shepard by ensuring that the Government protects and provides proper access to information to advance the national and public interest.

(CUI) For training purposes this paragraph contrails CUI. We lead efforts to standardize and assess the management of classified and controlled unclassified information through oversight, policy development, guidance, education, and reporting.

CONTROLLED

Department of Good Works
Washington, D.C. 20006

August 27, 2016

MEMORANDUM FOR THE DIRECTOR

From: Det. Jonathon McLane
NYPD Liaison Officer

Subject: (U) Examples

(U) We support President Shepard by ensuring that the Government protects and provides proper access to information to advance the national and public interest.

(CUI) For training purposes this paragraph contrails CUI Specified. We lead efforts to standardize and assess the management of classified and controlled unclassified information through oversight, policy development, guidance, education, and reporting.

(U) Markings informational only, not carried to CUI Banner

"Parenthetical" Portion Marking Examples

Portion Markings with Category Only (Reference 32 CFR 2002.20(f))

This example shows how to portion mark a document using the CUI Control Marking and CUI Category or Subcategory Markings. When a document contains CUI Specified, all CUI Specified Category or Subcategory Markings must be included in the CUI Banner Marking. Consult your agency CUI policy for guidance on the use of CUI Basic Category or Subcategory Markings. When CUI Portion Markings are used, and a portion does not contain CUI, a

"U" is placed in parentheses to indicate that the portion contains Uncontrolled-Unclassified Information.

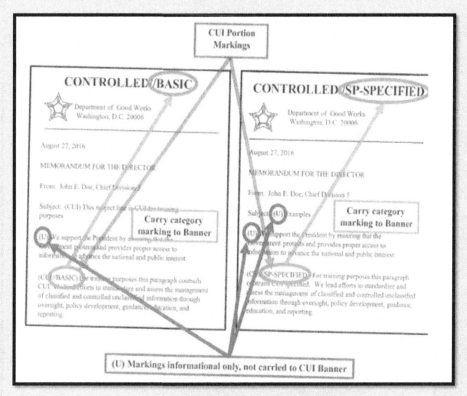

Portion Marking with Category Only

The above example uses "BASIC" and "SPECIFIED" as substitutes for CUI Category or Subcategory Markings. Consult the CUI Registry for actual CUI markings.

Portion Markings with Category and Dissemination Caveats (Reference 32 CFR 2002.20(f))

The example below shows how to portion mark a document using all three components of the CUI Banner Marking. When a document contains CUI Specified, CUI Specified Category or Subcategory Markings must be included in the CUI Banner Marking. Consult your agency CUI policy for guidance on the use of CUI Basic Category or Subcategory Markings. Also, when CUI Portion Markings are used, and a portion does not contain CUI, a "U" is placed in parentheses to indicate that the portion contains Uncontrolled-Unclassified Information.

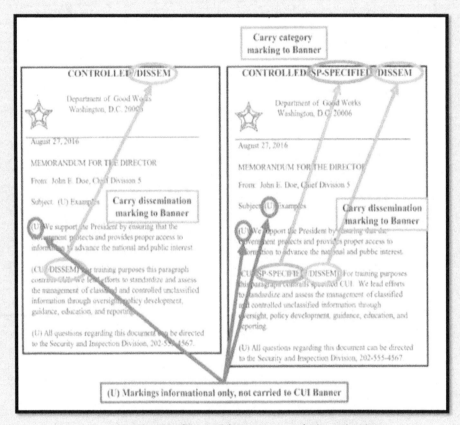

Portion Markings with Category and Dissemination

The above example uses "SP-SPECIFIED" as a substitute for a CUI Category or Subcategory Marking and "DISSEM" as a substitute for Limited Dissemination Control Markings. Consult the CUI Registry for actual CUI markings.

Common Mistakes in Banner Markings

Category and Subcategory Markings for CUI Specified MUST always be included in the Banner Marking, and those for CUI Basic may be required by agency CUI policy. When CUI Portion Markings are used and include CUI Category or Subcategory Markings, those markings MUST be included in the CUI Banner Marking.

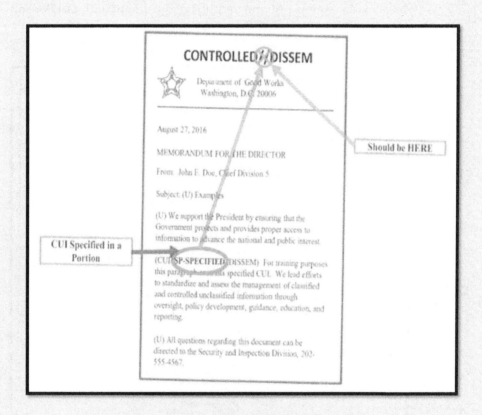

The above example uses "SP-SPECIFIED" as a substitute for a CUI Specified Category or Subcategory Marking and "DISSEM" as a substitute for a Limited Dissemination Control Marking. Consult the CUI Registry for actual CUI markings.

Marking of Multiple Pages (Reference 32 CFR 2002.20(c))

The composition of the CUI Banner Marking for a multi-page document is essentially the totality of all the CUI markings in the document; if any portion of the document contains CUI Specified or a Limited Dissemination Control Marking, then the CUI Banner Marking must reflect that.

Below is an example of one multi-page document with CUI Portion Marking.

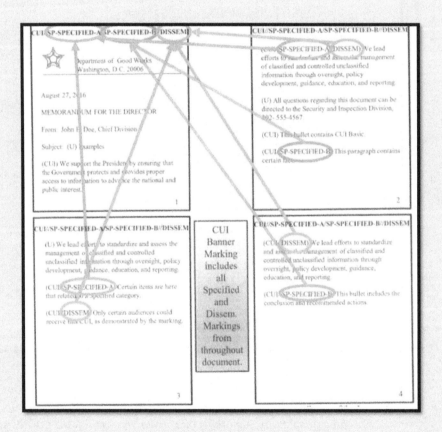

The overall CUI Banner Marking for the document must appear on all pages of the document.

Required Indicators as directed by Authorities (Reference 32 CFR 2002.20 (b)(2)(iii))

Required indicators that include informational, warning, or dissemination statements may be mandated by the law, Federal regulation, or Government-wide policy that makes a specific item of information CUI. These indicators shall not be included in the CUI Banner or portion markings but must appear in a manner readily apparent to authorized personnel. This shall be consistent with the requirements of the governing document.

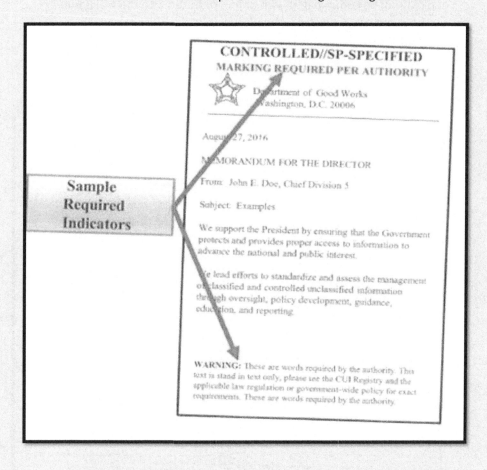

The above example uses "SPECIFIED" as a substitute for a CUI Specified Category or Subcategory Marking. Consult the CUI Registry for actual CUI markings.

Supplemental Administrative Markings (Reference 32 CFR 2002.20(l))

Agencies may use supplemental administrative markings (e.g., Draft, Deliberative, Pre- decisional, Provisional) along with CUI to inform recipients of the non-final status of documents ONLY when such markings are created and defined in agency policy.

Supplemental administrative markings may not be used to control CUI and may not be commingled with or incorporated into the CUI Banner Marking or Portion Markings. Supplemental administrative markings may not duplicate any marking in the CUI Registry.

Below are two examples of ways to properly use supplemental administrative markings.

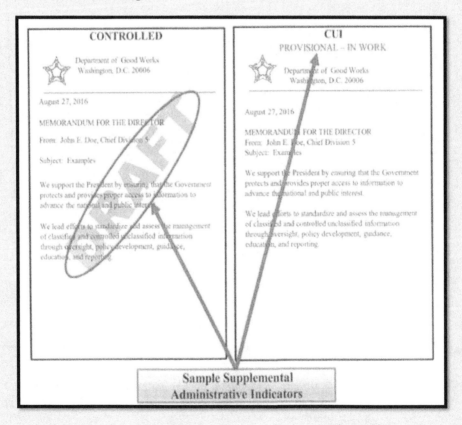

Common Mistakes for Supplemental Administrative Markings

Supplemental administrative markings may not be used to control CUI and must not be incorporated into CUI Banner Markings or CUI Portion Markings or duplicate any marking in the CUI Registry.

Below are two examples of ways **NOT** to use administrative markings.

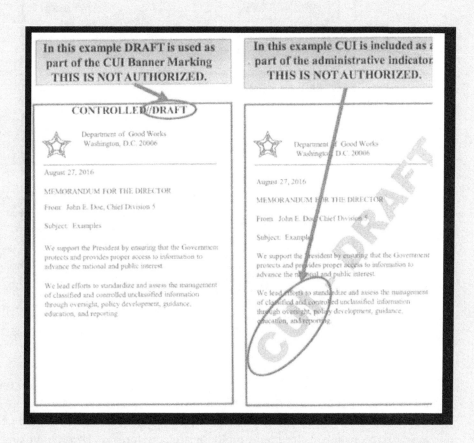

Electronic Media Storage and Marking Procedures (Reference 32 CFR 2002.20)

Media such as USB sticks, hard drives, and CD ROMs must be marked to alert CUI holders to the presence of CUI stored on the device. Due to space limitations, it may not be possible to include Category, Subcategory, or Limited Dissemination Control Markings on the given surface. At a minimum, mark media with the CUI Control Marking ("CONTROLLED" or "CUI") and the Designating Agency. Equipment can be marked or labeled to indicate that CUI is stored on the device.

Equipment can be marked or labeled to indicate that CUI is stored on the device.

NOTE: DOGW is an acronym for Department of Good Works.

Marking Forms (Reference 32 CFR 2002.20)

Forms that contain CUI must be marked when completed. If space on the form is limited, cover sheets can be used for this purpose. As forms are updated during agency implementation of the CUI Program, they should be modified to include a statement that indicates the form is CUI when finalized.

CUI Control Marking

CONTROLLED
when filled in

Standard Form 86
Revised December 2010
U.S. Office of Personnel Management
5 CFR Parts 731, 732, and 736

QUESTIONNAIRE FOR
NATIONAL SECURITY POSITIONS

Form approved:
OMB No. 3206-0005

PERSONS COMPLETING THIS FORM SHOULD BEGIN WITH THE QUESTIONS BELOW AFTER CAREFULLY READING THE PRECEDING INSTRUCTIONS.

I have read the instructions and I understand that if I withhold, misrepresent, or falsify information on this form, I am subject to the penalties for inaccurate or false statement (per U. S. Criminal Code, Title 18, section 1001), denial or revocation of a security clearance, and/or removal and debarment from Federal Service. ☐ YES ☐ NO

Section 1 - Full Name

Provide your full name. If you have only initials in your name, provide them and indicate "Initial only". If you do not have a middle name, indicate "No Middle Name". If you are a "Jr.," "Sr." etc. enter this under Suffix.

Last name	First name	Middle name	Suffix
BAUER	JACK	ALLEN	Sr

Section 2 - Date of Birth | **Section 3 - Place of Birth**

Provide your date of birth. (Month/Day/Year)
06/25/1969

Provide your place of birth
City: ANYWHERE   County: THIS COUNTY   State: AK   Country (Required): United States

Section 4 - Social Security Number

Provide your U.S. Social Security Number.
123-45-6789   ☐ Not applicable

Section 5 - Other Names Used

Have you used any other names?   ☐ YES ☒ NO (If NO, proceed to Section 6)

Complete the following if you have responded "Yes" to having used other names.

Provide your other name(s) used and the period of time you used them (for example: your maiden name(s), name(s) by a former marriage, former name(s), alias(es), or nickname(s)). If you have only initials in your name(s), provide them and indicate "Initial only". If you do not have a middle name (s), indicate "No Middle Name" (NMN). If you are a "Jr.," "Sr." etc. enter this under Suffix.

#1 Last name	First name	Middle name	Suffix

From (Month/Year)   To (Month/Year)   ☐ Present   Maiden name?   Provide the reason(s) why the name changed

CUI Coversheets (Reference 32 CFR 2002.32)

The use of CUI coversheets is optional except when required by agency policy. Agencies may download coversheets from the CUI Registry or obtain printed copies through the General Services Administration (GSA) Global Supply Centers or the GSAAdvantage online service (https://www.gsa.gov/buying-selling/purchasing-programs/requisition-programs/gsa-global-supply/easy-ordering/gsa-global-supply-online-ordering).

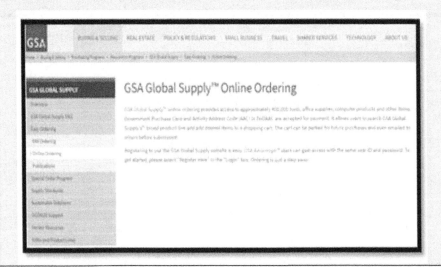

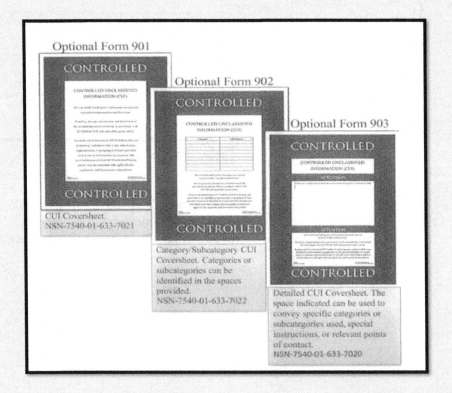

Optional Form 901

CUI Coversheet.
NSN-7540-01-633-7021

Optional Form 902

Category/Subcategory CUI
Coversheet. Categories or
subcategories can be
identified in the spaces
provided.
NSN-7540-01-633-7022

Optional Form 903

Detailed CUI Coversheet. The
space indicated can be used to
convey specific categories or
subcategories used, special
instructions, or relevant points
of contact.
NSN-7540-01-633-7020

Marking Transmittal Documents (Reference 32 CFR 2002.20)

When a transmittal document accompanies CUI, the transmittal document must indicate that CUI is attached or enclosed. The transmittal document must also include, conspicuously, the following or similar instructions, as appropriate:

- "When the enclosure is removed, this document is Uncontrolled- Unclassified Information"; or

- "When the enclosure is removed, this document is (CUI Control Level); or

- "Upon removal, this document does not contain CUI."

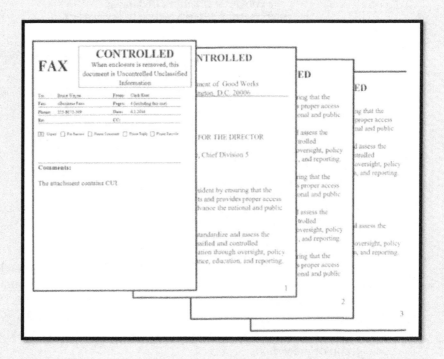

Alternate Marking Methods (Reference 32 CFR 2002.20)

Agency heads[7] may authorize the use of alternate marking methods on IT systems, websites, browsers, or databases through agency CUI policy. These may be used to alert users to the presence of CUI, where the agency head has issued a limited CUI marking waiver for CUI designated within the agency. These warnings may take multiple forms and include the examples below.

Computer Monitor CUI Banners

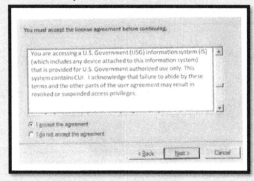

Agency or Company Legal Warning Notification

Room or Area Markings (Reference 32 CFR 2002.20)

In areas containing CUI, it may be necessary to alert personnel who are not authorized to access the area or information. This may be accomplished by any means approved by the agency and detailed in the agency's CUI policy. Typically, signs are posted exterior to the room or rooms, on all entry doors, and in any ante-room designated to verify clearances or need-to-know status of a group or individual.

---

[7] Agency Heads may be considered federal agency secretaries, leadership, etc., designated under contract to provide direct oversight of the agencies' CUI program.

Below is a sample of a sign that indicates CUI is present.

Example Exterior Door and Interior Rooms Sign

Container Markings (Reference 32 CFR 2002.20)

When an agency is storing CUI, authorized holders should mark the container to indicate that it contains CUI.

Below are some basic examples.

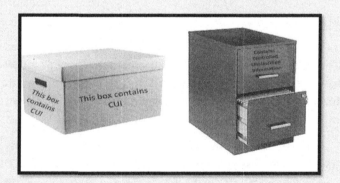

Shipping and Mailing (Reference 32 CFR 2002.20)

Agency heads must ensure that mailroom staffs are trained in handling CUI to include reporting any loss, theft, or misuse.

When shipping CUI:

- Address packages that contain CUI for delivery only to a specific recipient.

- DO NOT put CUI markings on the outside of an envelope or package for mailing/shipping.

- Use in-transit automated tracking and accountability tools where possible.

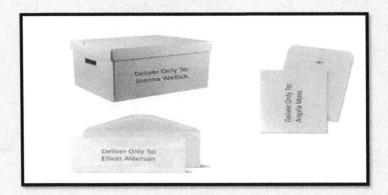

Re-marking Legacy Information (Reference 32 CFR 2002.36)

Legacy information is unclassified information that was marked as restricted from access or dissemination in some way or otherwise controlled before the CUI Program was established. **All legacy information is not automatically CUI.** Agencies must examine and determine what legacy information qualifies as CUI and mark it accordingly.

In cases of excessive burden, an agency's' head may issue a "Legacy Marking Waiver," as described in 32 CFR 2002.38(b) of the CUI Rule. When the agency head grants such a waiver, legacy material that qualifies need not be re-marked as CUI until and unless it is to be "re-used" in a new document.

LEGACY MARKING

 Department of Good Works
Washington, D.C. 20006

August 27, 2016

MEMORANDUM FOR THE DIRECTOR

From: John E. Doe, Chief Division 5

Subject: Examples

We support the President by ensuring that the Government
protects and provides proper access to information to
advance the national and public interest.

We lead efforts to standardize and assess the management
of classified and controlled unclassified information
through oversight, policy development, guidance,
education, and reporting.

"LEGACY MARKING" is used as a substitute for ad hoc, agency markings used to label unclassified information before the creation of the CUI Program.

When legacy information is to be re-used and incorporated into another document of any kind, it must undergo the process described below.

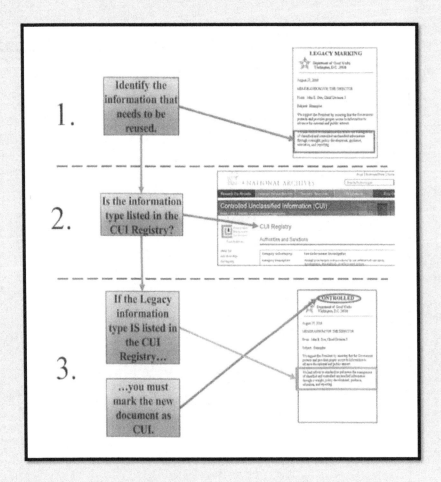

When possible, contact the originator of the information for guidance in remarking and protecting the legacy information in the CUI Program.

CUI MARKINGS IN A CLASSIFIED ENVIRONMENT

Marking Commingled Information (Reference 32 CFR 2002.20(g))

When CUI is included in a document that contains any classified information, that document is referred to as **commingled**. Commingled documents are subject to the requirements of the CUI and Classified National Security Information (CNSI) Programs. As a best practice, keep the CUI and classified information in separate and designated areas to the greatest extent possible[8]. Mark all portions to ensure that authorized holders can distinguish CUI portions from those containing CNSI or Uncontrolled-Unclassified Information; the de-controlling provisions for CUI apply only to portions marked as CUI. CNSI portions remain classified to their declassification requirements.

Executive Order 13526 - Classified National Security Information

In the overall marking banner's CUI section, double forward slashes (//) are used to separate significant elements, and single forward slashes (/) are

---

[8] Typically, classified facilities should be partitioned to include designated drawers, safes, and folders specific to CUI storage.

used to separate sub-elements. The CUI Control Marking ("CUI") appears in the overall banner marking directly before the CUI category and subcategory markings. When there is CUI Specified in the document, CUI Specified category and subcategory marking(s) must appear in the overall banner marking. Per agency policy, if used, the optional CUI Basic category and subcategory markings would appear next. Both CUI Specified and CUI Basic markings are separately alphabetized. The limited dissemination control markings apply to the entire document and the CUI and classified information in it. Placeholders are not used for missing elements or sub-elements.

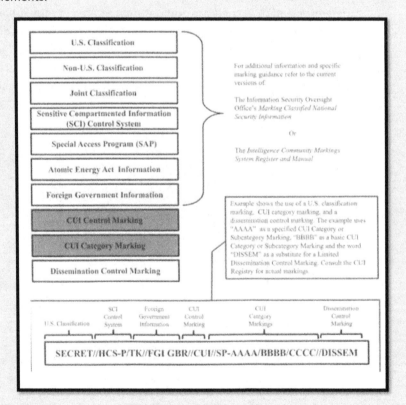

Commingling in the same paragraph is not recommended, where paragraphs contain CUI and CNSI commingled, portion marking elements follow a similar syntax to the banner marking. <u>However, the paragraph always takes the HIGHEST classification of the information contained in the paragraph</u>.

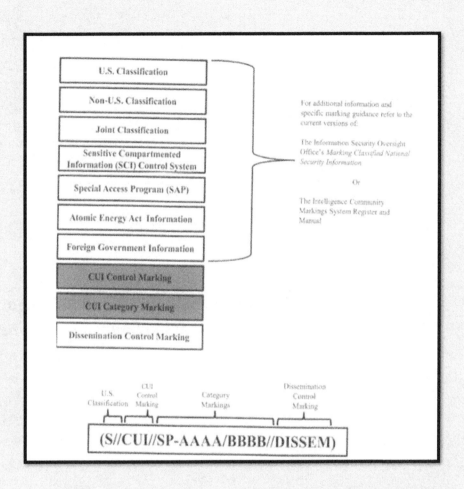

For additional information and specific marking, the guidance refers to the current versions of The Information Security Oversight Office's *Marking Classified National Security Information.*

Commingling Example 1

In cases where· CUI is commingled with classified information, the following applies:

- In banners, the CUI Control Marking is used only in its abbreviated form ("CUI"). The longer form ("CONTROLLED") is not used. Either the classification marking, CUI control marking ("CUI"), or the Uncontrolled Unclassified Marking ("U") must be used in every portion.

- Limited Dissemination Control Markings must appear in the banner line and in all portions to which they apply.

Best practice: CUI and CNSI should be placed in separate portions of a document

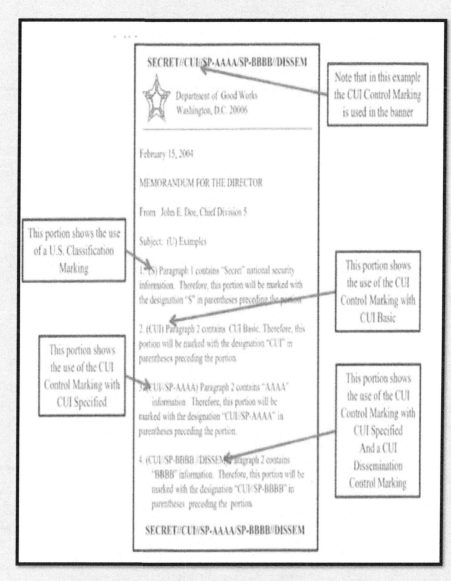

The above examples use "SP-AAAA" or "SP-BBBB" as CUI Specified Category or Subcategory Markings and the word "DISSEM" as a substitute for a Limited Dissemination Control Marking. Consult the CUI Registry for actual markings.

Commingling Example 2

These examples show the various ways CUI may be identified in a document.

SECRET//CUI

(U) Example of Slide Markings

• (CUI) This bullet contains "Controlled U
Information." Therefore, this portion will b
with the designation "CUI" in parentheses
the portion.
• (S) This bullet contains "Secret" informat
Therefore this portion will be marked with
designation "S" in parentheses preceding th

SECRET//CUI

SECRET//CUI//SP-AAAA/SP-BBBB//DISSEM

Department of Good Works
Washington, D.C. 20006

February 15, 2004

MEMORANDUM FOR THE DIRECTOR

From: John E. Doe, Chief Division 5

Subject: (U) Examples

1. (S) Paragraph 1 contains "Secret" national security information.
Therefore, this portion will be marked with the designation "S" in
parentheses preceding the portion.

2. (CUI/SP-AAAA) Paragraph 2 contains "AAAA"
information. Therefore, this portion will be marked with
the designation "CUI/SP-AAAA" in parentheses preceding the
portion.

3. (CUI/SP-BBBB//DISSEM) Paragraph 2 contains "BBBB"
information. Therefore, this portion will be
marked with the designation "CUI/SP-BBBB" in parentheses
preceding the portion.

SECRET//CUI//SP-AAAA/SP-BBBB//DISSEM

The above examples use "SP-AAAA" or "SP-BBBB" as CUI Specified Category or Subcategory Markings and the word "DISSEM" as a substitute for a Limited Dissemination Control Marking. Consult the CU Registry for actual markings.

Commingling Example 3

Below are two samples of CUI commingled with classified information, specifically with Classified National Security Information (CNSI). The sample on the left has the CUI and CNSI broken into separate paragraphs allowing for more natural future separation when needed to accommodate differing access requirements. The sample on the right has CUI and CNSI in the same paragraph.

The above examples use the word "SP-AAAA" as a substitute for a CUI Specified Category or Subcategory Marking. Consult the CUI Registry for actual markings.

Commingling Portion Markings (Reference 32 CFR 2002.20(g))

In a commingled document, when a portion contains both CUI and classified information, the portion marking for the classified information must precede the CUI Portion Marking. When commingling CUI with classified information, the user should retain the CUI, and classified portions separate to the greatest extent possible to allow for maximum information sharing. Many of the intricate markings seen below can be avoided by following this simple practice. Below are some examples of how to mark portions containing CUI.

Portion Marking	Contents of Portions Marked Section – CUI ONLY IN PORTION
(CUI)	This section contains CUI Basic.
(CUI//AAAA)	This section contains CUI Basic (with optional category marking).
(CUI/SP-BBBB)	This section contains CUI Specified.
(CUI/SP-BBBB/SP-CCCC)	This section contains two CUI Specified Categories in alphabetical order.
(CUI//DISSEM)	This section contains CUI Basic with a Limited Dissemination Control Marking
(CUI//AAAA//DISSEM)	This section contains CUI Basic with a Limited Dissemination Control Marking
(CUI/SP-BBBB//DISSEM)	This section contains CUI Specified with a Limited Dissemination Control Marking.
Portion Marking	**Contents of Portions Marked Section – WITH COMMINGLED PORTIONS (NOT RECOMMENDED)**
(S//CUI)	This section contains Secret information and CUI Basic.
(S//CUI//AAAA)	This section contains Secret information and CUI Basic (with optional category marking).
(S//CUI/SP-BBBB)	This section contains Secret information and CUI Specified.
(S//CUI/SP-BBBB/SP-CCCC)	This section contains Secret information and contains two CUI Specified Categories in alphabetical order.
(S//CUI/SP-BBBB//DISSEM)	This section contains Secret information and CUI Specified with a Limited Dissemination Control Marking.

Audit log.   A chronological record of information system activities, including records of system accesses and operations performed in a given period.

Authentication.   Verifying the identity of a user, process, or device, often as a prerequisite to allowing access to resources in an information system.

Availability.   Ensuring timely and reliable access to and use of information.

Baseline Configuration. A documented set of specifications for an information system, or a configuration item within a system, that has been formally reviewed and agreed on at a given point in time, and which can be changed only through change control procedures.

Blacklisting.   The process used to identify: (i) software programs that are not authorized to execute on an information system; or (ii) prohibited websites.

Confidentiality.   Preserving authorized restrictions on information access and disclosure, including means for protecting personal privacy and proprietary information.

Configuration Management. A collection of activities focused on establishing and maintaining the integrity of information technology products and information systems, through control of processes for initializing, changing, and monitoring the configurations of those products and systems throughout the system development life cycle.

Controlled Unclassified Information (CUI/FCI/CDI).

                            Information that law, regulation, or governmentwide policy requires to have safeguarding or disseminating controls, excluding information that is classified under Executive Order 13526, Classified National Security Information, December 29, 2009, or any predecessor or successor order, or the Atomic Energy Act of 1954, as amended.

External network.   A network not controlled by the company or agency.

FIPS-validated cryptography.   A cryptographic module validated by the Cryptographic Module Validation Program (CMVP) to meet requirements specified in FIPS Publication 140-2 (as amended). As a prerequisite to CMVP validation, the cryptographic module is required to employ a cryptographic algorithm implementation that has successfully passed validation testing by the Cryptographic Algorithm Validation Program (CAVP).

Hardware.   The physical components of an information system.

Incident.   An occurrence that actually or potentially jeopardizes the confidentiality, integrity, or availability of an information system or the information the system processes, stores, or transmits or that constitutes a violation or imminent threat of violation of security policies, security procedures, or acceptable use policies.

Information Security.   The protection of information and information systems from unauthorized access, use, disclosure, disruption, modification, or destruction to provide confidentiality, integrity, and availability.

Information System.   A discrete set of information resources organized for the collection, processing, maintenance, use, sharing, dissemination, or disposition of information.

Information Technology.   Any equipment or interconnected system or subsystem of equipment that is used in the automatic acquisition, storage, manipulation, management, movement, control, display, switching, interchange, transmission, or reception of data or information by the executive agency. It includes computers, ancillary equipment, software, firmware, and similar procedures, services (including support services), and related resources.

Integrity.   Guarding against improper information modification or destruction and includes ensuring information non-repudiation and authenticity.

Internal Network.   A network where: (i) the establishment, maintenance, and provisioning of security controls are under the direct control of organizational employees or contractors; or (ii) cryptographic encapsulation or similar security technology implemented between organization-controlled endpoints, provides the same effect (at least concerning confidentiality and integrity).

Malicious Code.   Software intended to perform an unauthorized process that will hurt the confidentiality, integrity, or availability of an information system; a virus, worm, Trojan horse, or other code-based entity that infects a host. Spyware and some forms of adware are also examples of malicious code.

Media.   Physical devices or writing surfaces including, but not limited to, magnetic tapes, optical disks, magnetic disks, and printouts (but not including display media) onto which information is recorded, stored, or printed within an information system.

Mobile Code.   Software programs or parts of programs obtained from remote information systems, transmitted across a network, and executed on a local information system without explicit installation or execution by the recipient.

Mobile device.   A portable computing device that: (i) has a small form factor such that a single individual can easily carry it; (ii) is designed to operate without a physical connection (e.g., wirelessly transmit or receive information); (iii) possesses local, nonremovable or removable data storage; and (iv) includes a self-contained power source. Mobile devices may also include voice communication capabilities, on-board sensors that allow the devices to capture information or built-in features for synchronizing local data with remote locations. Examples include smartphones, tablets, and E-readers.

Multifactor Authentication. Authentication using two or more different factors to achieve authentication. Factors include: (i) something you know (e.g., password/PIN); (ii) something you have (e.g., cryptographic identification device, token); or (iii) something you are (e.g., biometric).

Nonfederal Information System. An information system that does not meet the criteria for a federal information system. Nonfederal organization.

Network.   Information system(s) implemented with a collection of interconnected components. Such components may include routers, hubs, cabling, telecommunications controllers, key distribution centers, and technical control devices.

Portable storage device.	An information system component that can be inserted into and removed from an information system, and that is used to store data or information (e.g., text, video, audio, or image data). Such components are typically implemented on magnetic, optical, or solid-state devices (e.g., floppy disks, compact/digital video disks, flash/thumb drives, external hard disk drives, and flash memory cards/drives that contain nonvolatile memory).
Privileged Account.	An information system account with authorizations of a privileged user.
Privileged User.	A user that is authorized (and therefore, trusted) to perform security-relevant functions that ordinary users are not authorized to perform.
Remote Access.	Access to an organizational information system by a user (or a process acting on behalf of a user) communicating through an external network (e.g., the Internet).
Risk.	A measure of the extent to which a potential circumstance or event threaten an entity, and typically a function of (i) the adverse impacts that would arise if the circumstance or event occurs; and (ii) the likelihood of occurrence. Information system-related security risks are those risks that arise from the loss of confidentiality, integrity, or availability of information or information systems and reflect the potential adverse impacts to organizational operations (including mission, functions, image, or reputation), organizational assets, individuals, other organizations, and the Nation.
Sanitization.	Actions were taken to render data written on media unrecoverable by both ordinary and, for some forms of sanitization, extraordinary means. The process of removing information from media such that data recovery is not possible. It includes removing all classified labels, markings, and activity logs.
Security Control.	A safeguard or countermeasure prescribed for an information system or an organization designed to protect the confidentiality, integrity, and availability of its information and to meet a set of defined security requirements.

Security Control Assessment. The testing or evaluation of security controls to determine the extent to which the controls are implemented correctly, operating as intended, and producing the desired outcome concerning meeting the security requirements for an information system or organization.

Security Functions. The hardware, software, or firmware of the information system responsible for enforcing the system security policy and supporting the isolation of code and data on which the protection is based.

Threat. Any circumstance or event with the potential to adversely impact organizational operations (including mission, functions, image, or reputation), organizational assets, individuals, other organizations, or the Nation through an information system via unauthorized access, destruction, disclosure, modification of information, or denial of service.

Whitelisting. The process used to identify: (i) software programs that are authorized to execute an information system.

MAJOR SUPPORTING REFERENCES

CNSSI 1253, *Security Categorization and Control Selection for National Security Systems*, 27 March 2014.

DoDI 8510.01, *Risk Management Framework for DoD Information Technology*, March 12, 2014 (and Change 1 effective 24 May 2016).

Executive Order 12958, as Amended, Classified National Security Information.

Executive Order 13556, *Controlled Unclassified Information*, November 2010.
http://www.gpo.gov/fdsys/pkg/FR-2010-11-09/pdf/2010-28360.pdf

Executive Order 13636, *Improving Critical Infrastructure Cybersecurity*, February 2013.
http://www.gpo.gov/fdsys/pkg/FR-2013-02-19/pdf/2013-03915.pdf

Federal Information Security Modernization Act of 2014 (P.L. 113-283), December 2014.
http://www.gpo.gov/fdsys/pkg/PLAW-113publ283/pdf/PLAW-113publ283.pdf

National Institute of Standards and Technology (NIST) Federal Information Processing Standards Publication 200 (as amended), *Minimum Security Requirements for Federal Information and Information Systems*.
http://csrc.nist.gov/publications/fips/fips200/FIPS-200-final-march.pdf

National Institute of Standards and Technology Special Publication 800-53A Revision 4, *Assessing Security and Privacy Controls in Federal Information Systems and Organizations*, December 2014 (and 18 December 2014 updates)

National Institute of Standards and Technology Special Publication 800-53 Revision 4, *Security and Privacy Controls for Federal Information Systems and Organizations*, April 2013 (and 22 January 2015 updates).

National Institute of Standards and Technology Special Publication 800-53 (as amended), *Security and Privacy Controls for Federal Information Systems and Organizations*.
http://dx.doi.org/10.6028/NIST.SP.800-53r4

National Institute of Standards and Technology Special Publication 800-171, rev. 1, *Protecting Controlled Unclassified Information in Nonfederal Information Systems and Organizations*. https://nvlpubs.nist.gov/nistpubs/SpecialPublications/NIST.SP.800-171r1.pdf

National Institute of Standards and Technology Special Publication 800-171A, *Assessing Security Requirements for Controlled Unclassified Information*
https://csrc.nist.gov/CSRC/media/Publications/sp/800-171a/draft/sp800-171A-draft.pdf

National Institute of Standards and Technology *Framework for Improving Critical Infrastructure Cybersecurity* (as amended).
http://www.nist.gov/cyberframework

SELECTED ACRONYMS

AA	Assessment and Authorization
AO	Authorizing Official
ATO	Authorization to Operate
CIO	Chief Information Officer
DCIO	Deputy Chief Information Officer
IAW	In accordance with
IASE	Information Assurance Security Engineer
IPT	Integrated Product Team
ISSE	Information Systems Security Engineer
ISSM	Information System Security Manager
ISSO	Information System Security Officer
JPO	Joint Program Office
JSIG	Joint Special Access Program Implementation Guide
NIST	National Institute of Standards and Technology
OCIO	Office of the Chief Information Officer
RMF	Risk Management Framework
SABI	Secret and Below Information
SCA	Security Controls Assessor
STIG	Security Technical Implementation Guidance

ABOUT THE AUTHOR

Mr. Russo is the former Senior Information Security Engineer within the Department of Defense's (DOD) F-35 Joint Strike Fighter program. He has an extensive background in cybersecurity and is an expert in the Risk Management Framework (RMF) and DOD Instruction 8510, which implements RMF throughout the DOD and the federal government. He holds both a Certified Information Systems Security Professional (CISSP) certification and a CISSP in information security architecture (ISSAP). He holds a 2017 certification as a Chief Information Security Officer (CISO) from the National Defense University, Washington, DC. He retired from the US Army Reserves in 2012 as the Senior Intelligence Officer.

He is the former CISO at the Department of Education, wherein 2016; he led the effort to close over 95% of the outstanding US Congressional and Inspector General cybersecurity shortfall weaknesses spanning as far back as five years.

Mr. Russo is the former Senior Cybersecurity Engineer supporting the Joint Medical Logistics Development Functional Center of the Defense Health Agency (DHA) at Fort Detrick, MD. He led a team of engineering and cybersecurity professionals protecting five major Medical Logistics systems supporting over 200 DOD Medical Treatment Facilities around the globe.

In 2011, Mr. Russo was certified by the Office of Personnel Management as a graduate of the Senior Executive Service Candidate program.

From 2009 through 2011, Mr. Russo was the Chief Technology Officer at the Small Business Administration (SBA). He led a team of over 100 IT professionals in supporting an intercontinental Enterprise IT infrastructure and security operations spanning 12-time zones; he deployed cutting-edge technologies to enhance SBA's business and information sharing operations supporting the small business community. Mr. Russo was the first-ever Program Executive Officer (PEO)/Senior Program Manager in the Office of Intelligence & Analysis at Headquarters, Department of Homeland Security (DHS), Washington, DC. Mr. Russo was responsible for the development and deployment of secure Information and Intelligence support systems for OI&A to include software applications and systems to enhance the DHS mission. He was responsible for the program management development lifecycle during his tenure at DHS.

He holds a Master of Science from the National Defense University in Government Information Leadership with a concentration in Cybersecurity and a Bachelor of Arts in Political Science with a minor in Russian Studies from Lehigh University. He holds Level III Defense Acquisition certification in Program Management, Information Technology, and Systems Engineering. He has been a member of the DOD Acquisition Corps since 2001.

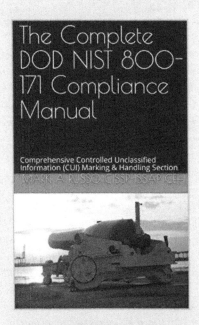

<u>NOTES</u>

NOTES

Made in the USA
Coppell, TX
03 June 2022

78432594R00037